Steam Memories: 1950's – 1960's

No. 20: NORTH EAST SCRAP

Including: *Clayton Davie, Hughes, Bolckows, W. Willoughby, Darlington Works
Arnott Young & Thompsons*

Copyright Book Law Publications 2010
ISBN 978-1-907094-92-7

INTRODUCTION

As a request from Publisher David Allen at Book Law, following a good response from my first book North Eastern Scrapyards, a second volume has come about because a wealth of material has surfaced since the publication of Volume 1. Various photographers have been kind enough to supply me with their negatives and I am eternally grateful to them. Since Volume 1 another two yards have now been featured – Thompsons of Stockton and the Arnott Young facility at Fighting Cocks, Dinsdale.

My special thanks go to the photographers who have through their foresight created this railway historic record with their super images. I am indebted especially to David J.Dippie, a brilliant craftsman for his assistance with his captions and photographic knowledge – Thank you David. Not forgetting Peter J.Robinson (Tynemouth), Mel Rutter and Bob Anderson (Bedlington), Ian S.Carr (Sunderland), Barry Nicholson (Harraton), and the late J.W.Armstrong and Keith Gregory, courtesy of Alan Thompson (Armstrong Photographic Trust), Ian H.B.Lewis (Scarborough), courtesy of Peter Freund, Walter P.Hodgson, courtesy of Eric Colling and finally Eric Wilson courtesy, of Alan Brooks.

Howard Forster receives thanks from me for diligently proof reading the captions.

To my beautiful wife Judith for putting up with me and my obsession, and being a 'computer widow' – Thank you.

David Dunn, Cramlington, July 2010.

(*previous page*) **Hughes, Bolckow, North Blyth. This nearly complete BR Standard 9F 2-10-0 No.92179, fitted with a BR1F high sided tender, had been allocated to New England when new, and withdrawn from Langwith Junction prior to storage at Colwick, before making its final journey to the North East, and oblivion. This cold, late February, day in 1966, shows the mighty 9F's form to great effect, sandwiched between a pair of Thompson B1.** *M.Rutter.*

Printed and bound by The Amadeus Press, Cleckheaton, West Yorkshire
First published in the United Kingdom by Book Law Publications, 382 Carlton Hill, Nottingham, NG4 1JA

Having arrived from storage at Hull Dairycoates, D49/2 'Hunt' No.62760 THE COTSWOLD is complete apart from the cast foxes missing from both nameplates. We have quite a nice view showing the Lentz Rotary Cam Poppet gear to good effect as captured by the camera of 14 years old David J.Dippie. This was David's first photograph in North Road scrapyard, taken on 26th October 1959. The D49/2 was a locomotive type rarely seen in his home town of Sunderland, therefore this was a good opportunity to view them closely. D49s were seen in the early fifties on running-in turns from the works, usually on Darlington-Newcastle stopping trains. *D.J.Dippie.*

Sandwiched between Class T1 No.69913 and B16/1 No.61430 on the same day – 26th October 1959 – is D49/1 'Shire' No.62722 HUNTINGDONSHIRE which had been withdrawn from Hull Dairycoates shed six days earlier, and was shown as officially disposed of by 31st December 1959. The locomotive was complete including name, number, works and shed plates, also fitted unusually with a LNER Group Standard flared-top tender, Shires were normally fitted with ex Great Central tenders. One of these nameplates, which were cast in yellow brass at Darlington when the D49/1 was new on 10th July 1928, was sold to a collector at auction for £16,000 in 2002. The 'Shire' nameplates were cast with slightly softer metal than that used on some later classes, and a number of plates cracked vertically across the end boltholes, necessitating re-welding or replacement. Note the word 'scrap' chalked on the cab side, and the remains of a cab roof resting on top of the wheel sets in the foreground. The tenders were usually still full of coal, and mounds of this had to be regularly cleared from the yard. *D.J.Dippie.*

D49/2 'Hunt' No.62738 THE ZETLAND separated from its tender and D49/1 'Shire' No.62707 LANCASHIRE with a GC tender awaiting the cutters torch on the dismantling road. The ZETLAND, named after a hunt which met in South Durham & North Yorkshire, was withdrawn from York shed on 21st September 1959. All of the plates are still in situ although both forward facing brass foxes have been removed, either by souvenir hunters, or the works, to enable the sale of complete nameplates and foxes to collectors for the scrap value £3-£7. The left hand fox turned up at auction in September 2007 and the auction catalogue included the narrative 'Stored & scrapped at Darlington Works from where it was acquired by a railway man who took it home for his daughter who was interested in hunting and horses. For the past 48 years it has been used as a door stop, by the back door of their cottage.' Although almost all D49 nameplates are known to have survived, whether with original or works replacement foxes, very few smokebox numberplates have survived, presumably because the cast iron was seen as comparatively unattractive. Those that have survived now change hands for between £1,000 and £3,000 depending on whether they have been re-welded (for many were thrown down from the locomotive and fractured) or survived intact. No.62707 LANCASHIRE, behind No.62738 was withdrawn from Hull Dairycoates three weeks earlier on 6th October 1959. Both locomotives had been disposed of five days after this photograph was taken, after working lives of 27 years for the 'Hunt' and 31 years for the 'Shire'. To the right of 2738's bufferbeam lie the remains of an A5 4-6-2Ts cab. *D.J.Dippie.*

5

There are four Class A8 4-6-2Ts still intact in this photograph taken on 9th July 1960. Around the main subject, No.69880, are the other three, Nos.69861, 69850 and 69894. It was often North Road's practice to deal with locos from the same class, as they were often withdrawn together, when their working diagrams were handed over to classes of locomotives deemed more suitable in terms of age, condition or route availability; or finally to diesel locomotives and multiple units. No.69880 was withdrawn from West Hartlepool shed just ten days earlier, and would be disposed of within three weeks. Its' final duties would have included hauling non-corridor stock between Teeside, Newcastle, and Darlington. Designed by Vincent Raven for the North Eastern Railway in 1913 as Class D 4-4-4Ts, and rebuilt by Nigel Gresley as 4-6-2T for the LNER between 1933 and 1936 at Darlington works, these 86 ton workhorses had a working life of almost 30 years in rebuilt form. Notice the three types of coal bunker carried by the class: hopper, intermediate and small. *D.J.Dippie.*

A nice rear view of J21 class 0-6-0 No.65110 showing detail rarely seen in photographs. Rebuilt from an original North Eastern Railway design introduced by T.W.Worsdell in 1886, this engine has undergone a number of modifications during its lifetime of hauling mainly coal from the collieries in the North East, and passenger trains over cross-country routes such as Stainmore. No.65033 is the only survivor of the class, having utilised parts from the penultimate survivor No.65099. The preserved engine is currently at Shildon awaiting restoration, having initially worked at the North East open air museum at Beamish following its withdrawal and repainting in NER livery. For many years No.65110 worked as carriage pilot at Heaton shed until withdrawal. *D.J.Dippie.*

Looking in quite a sorry state, Class J25 0-6-0 No.65666 languishes in the rear storage line at North Road scrap yard, and will be shunted to one of the dismantling lines nearest to North Road station as space becomes available. Rebuilt by Vincent Raven from an 1898 design by Wilson Worsdell for the North Eastern Railway, and withdrawn from Hull Dairycoates shed, the locomotive has arrived minus coupling rods and its middle set of wheels, suggesting wear or damage either in storage or on its final Hull to Darlington journey. *D.J.Dippie.*

The 7.00 p.m. evening sun highlights the remarkably clean condition of A8 class 4-6-2T No.69880 which is standing in one of the two breaking lines. This is Saturday 9th July 1960, and as breaking up at North Road yard did not normally take place at weekends, the locomotive had only one more day before being attacked by the cutters torch. No.69880 was withdrawn from West Hartlepool just ten days earlier, and would be recorded on Works records as having been totally disposed of within three weeks. As a North Eastern enthusiast, it would have been wonderful to see one of these competent Gresley rebuilds working in preservation. *D.J.Dippie.*

Just in front of the engine in the previous photograph (page 9), standing in the breaking line, both in very clean external condition, with evidence of cleaning on the tank sides, we have A8s Nos.69894 and 69880, both had been withdrawn from West Hartlepool ten days earlier on the 30th June and cut up by 31st July. A number of the A8 class had been overhauled at Darlington in the late 50s' but on returning to their home depots were immediately put into storage, hence the reason why many of them arrived at the scrap yard looking remarkably clean compared to most other arrivals. Behind the A8s, the remains of the bunker of G5 0-4-4T No.67325 have been added to one of the metal stacks which were regularly removed to commercial recyclers. The G5 was withdrawn in October 1958, so it lay around for quite a while before its eventual removal. *D.J.Dippie.*

On 10th September 1960, A8's Nos.69860 and 69869 stand on one of the three storage lines at the back of North Road, both engines were withdrawn on 30th June from Thornaby. These too had been designed by Vincent Raven for the NER in 1913 as Class D 4-4-4Ts, then rebuilt by Nigel Gresley as Pacific tanks for the LNER between 1933 and 1936. The domes, chimneys, boiler cladding and smokeboxes varied amongst different locomotives. There were also three varieties of coal bunkers, the smallest and intermediate sizes of which can be seen here. When one of two breaking up lines at the front of the yard becomes vacant, they will be transferred there and finally disposed of by the end of the month. *D.J.Dippie.*

Having travelled from its home shed at Scarborough to North Road, A8 class No.69885 lies at the back of the yard awaiting removal to one of the cutting lines at the front, adjacent to North Road passenger station. On Saturday 10th September 1960, a visit to the scrap yard meant that access to the locomotives was always possible, with no apparent security or fencing in place. Note that the opened smokebox door shows a wealth of detail not normally seen. The A8 had been withdrawn on 30th June, and would cease to exist in another three weeks time. Its former stamping ground would have included the holiday resorts of the east coast of Yorkshire as well as the now privately owned North Yorkshire Moors railway. *D.J.Dippie.*

The handsome lines of Vincent Raven's original North Eastern Railway design of 1919 can be seen in B16/1 class No.61440 as it lies in one of the three storage lines at North Road awaiting movement to one of the breaking lines. Built at Darlington in 1923 as No.2369, it was one of a class of 70 locomotives of which 69 survived into BR days. (Although the unfortunate No.925 was destroyed in an air raid on York in April 1942, its frame survived and was used for the first Thompson rebuild of the class to B16/3. As a result, the frames and wheels from the last locomotive to be converted – 61434 – remained in Darlington Works yard for several years afterwards.) No.61440 has many similarities with Raven's earlier Pacific design of 1922, the erstwhile A2. The A2 class had of course, two trailing wheels, larger boiler and coupled wheels, and were, incidentally, cut up in this same yard. As flagships of the NER the 'City' class were named after five cities situated within what was to become the NER Region of BR – basically the old NER territory. Sadly neither class, B16 nor A2 survived into preservation. The rear coupling rods had probably been removed at shed and are still tied to the running plate. There is evidence of some enthusiastic attention to the smokebox door and numberplate before it was withdrawn from York on 31st July. The engine is recorded as having been totally broken up by 30th November 1960. The J94 No.68022, standing in front of the B16, shows the Gorton style of livery with the number on the bunker. *D.J.Dippie.*

13

The ex War Department and Riddles designed 'Austerity' saddle tanks were built in 1943 and after having been purchased in 1946 by the LNER and classified J94, Nos.68076 and 68022 became BR property but now stand some fourteen years later awaiting their fate on the North Road cutting line. The 40E shed code indicates the locomotive was withdrawn from Colwick. On the smokebox numberplate the early curly '6' should have been replaced with the Gill sans style as painted on the saddle tank. Note the chalked destination on the bunker SCRAP YARD – quite final. *D.J.Dippie.*

This J71, No.68316, is from a class introduced by T.W.Worsdell in 1886 for the NER. They were built at Darlington between 1886 and 1895. The first withdrawals began in 1933 during the slump in world trade. Our subject here was the very last of the class to be built, in November 1895, but was withdrawn from Borough Gardens shed in early October 1960, not quite sixty-five years old. The final survivor of the class, No.68233, was withdrawn in February 1961. These 0-6-0Ts were used throughout the North Eastern Region for shunting coaching stock, goods wagons and moving locomotives on shed. On this Saturday 22nd October 1960 the sun shines at 11.30 a.m. on a peaceful yard, which will begin breaking activities again in two days time on Monday morning. *D.J.Dippie.*

Edward Fletcher introduced his 0-4-4BTP (Bogie Tank Passenger) locomotives in 1874 for the North Eastern Railway, and Wilson Worsdell began rebuilding them some twenty-five years later into Class J77. This particular locomotive, No.68410, was built at Gateshead in 1877, rebuilt at York in 1900 and withdrawn from West Hartlepool earlier in the month when this photo taken around mid-day on a sunny Saturday 22nd October 1960, before the entire class became extinct just four months later. It retains the Fletcher round-topped cab, unlike some class members which were converted to the Worsdell square-cornered type. The bunker has been emptied and the ash removed from the smokebox, before moving it to one of North Road's two breaking tracks. These were nearest to North Road station in the background, and the long-gone British Road Services depot. A shovel lies on top of the tank, and the engine retains oblong deep sandboxes and leading springs above the footplate. One of its twin whistles is still attached to the cab roof. Just above the opened smokebox door can be seen the bodies of two grounded sentinel shunting locomotives, Nos.68149 and 68180, which became semi-permanent fixtures of the yard until its closure. *D.J.Dippie.*

This view, taken at 11.35 a.m. on Saturday 22nd October 1960, is of one of the three storage lines and is facing north-west, showing from left to right: J77 No.68410, J71s Nos.68316 and 68269, and J26 65777. The rail entrance to the scrapyard is directly ahead, and joins the Darlington to Heighington and Shildon line, shortly after North Road passenger station which is situated behind the trees on the right. This location is a stones throw from where the last built Peppercorn Pacific, No.60163 TORNADO was completed in 2008 at Hopetown Carriage works, located to the left of the picture. The three tank locomotives were designed or rebuilt by the Worsdells; T.W.Worsdell was Chief Mechanical Engineer of the NER between 1885 and 1890, followed by Wilson Worsdell from 1890 to 1910. Walking around the yard here had to be undertaken with care, even at weekends when no dismantling took place, because of the scrap components littered around. Eat your heart out 'Elf and Safety'. *D.J.Dippie.*

Another inmate of the yard on that Saturday, 22nd October 1960, was former NER Class C, now LNER/BR J72 No.68676 which lay beyond redemption. Its chimney, dome cover, cab and boiler cladding have been removed, but the firebox asbestos lagging is still in place and exposed! The BR workforce here, as in most places at that time, were unaware of the associated health problems whilst handling asbestos in any form. The brass cab fittings have also been removed from the backhead. A stencilled number 8296 on the boiler indicates that it had been used on a J71 withdrawn two years earlier. Both classes used the Diagram 73 boiler rated at 140 p.s.i. The 9in. x 5in. worksplate screwed to the bunker side will either find its way to the scrap stores at Darlington works for resale to a collector, or simply end up melted down. No.68676 was the seventh locomotive built in a class numbering 113. The first ten were built in 1898, and the final eight in 1951!, a testimony to their usefulness. They were built at Darlington, Doncaster and by the private contractor Armstrong Whitworth from a Wilson Worsdell design for the North Eastern Railway. Like the earlier and less powerful J71 tank engines, they were used throughout the North Eastern and Scottish regions for shunting freight in sidings and carriages at stations. Newcastle and York stations had No.68723 and 68736 painted in apple green livery with both NER and BR crests. Preserved No.69023 has the final version of this hybrid livery and is currently based ten miles from North Road at Shildon. *D.J.Dippie.*

An excellent photograph of another J71, No.68269, with J26 No.65777. The latter was withdrawn from Thornaby shed during September 1960 after a working life of almost 55 years, and is stabled on one of the three North Road storage lines awaiting removal to one of the two breaking lines. It has been separated from its tender, and has had its centre wheel set and connecting rod removed; possibly to save Thornaby's fitters the time and cost of repairing or replacing a worn axlebox before its last journey from Teesside. The locomotive crews certainly appreciated the protection afforded by the North Eastern cab, which at the time of locomotive's design by Wilson Worsdell in 1904, was far better than those fitted to locomotives of many other companies. Twenty-three of the twenty-five J26's remaining at the start of 1960 were based at Thornaby, the other two being at West Auckland. For their last twenty years the engines allocated to Thornaby shed worked mineral trains to the Teesside steelworks or headed into open country to the Kilton and Lingdale ironstone mines. Look at the wealth of backhead detail, invaluable to the railway modeller, especially with the roof partially cut away, also the rope tied to the handrail possibly holding the missing coupling rods. *D.J.Dippie.*

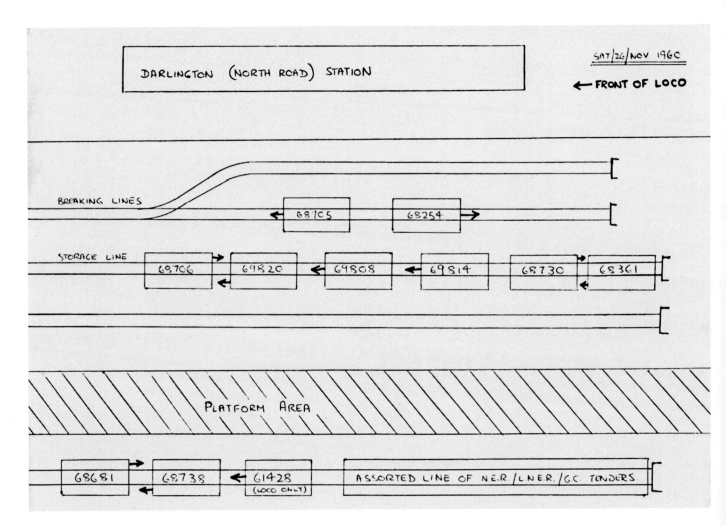

A hand drawn diagram of the situation at Darlington North Road scrapyard on Saturday 26th November 1960, showing the layout of the yard and the position of all the locomotives therein. *D.J.Dippie.*

J73 No.68361 stands in one of North Road's storage lines in the pouring rain at 12.25 p.m. on Saturday, 26th November 1960. This small class of just ten tank engines was designed by Wilson Worsdell in 1891. Built at Gateshead works for the NER, they were all delivered within seven months. The class was in service for between 57 and 68 years, No.68361 being the last to succumb when it was withdrawn from Hull Dairycoates. The smokebox locking bar has been removed to simplify removal of the ash, and has been left on the front footplating whilst a firing shovel lies on top of the side tank. It is fitted with Ross pop safety valves. There are three A5s and a J72 in front of the 0-6-0T, and when these have been disposed of No.68361 will follow them. (see illustration of yard layout on 26th November 1960). *DJ Dippie.*

North Road's common practice of dismantling batches of locomotives from the same class is illustrated in this line up of J.G. Robinson's former Great Central 4-6-2 tank locomotives designed for suburban traffic from Marylebone terminus. Visible in the previous illustration, these are the last three surviving A5s, and were withdrawn earlier in the month; No.69820 from Immingham, and Nos.69808 and 69814 from Colwick. All were withdrawn after operating suburban passenger trains of up to ten bogies throughout the ex-Great Central network for between 45 and 49 years. Both the LNER and GCR works plates are still in place, recording that all three engines were built at Manchester's Gorton works. Taken in pouring rain, only an enthusiastic 15 year-old would rest his camera on a piece of scrap machinery to give this photograph a two second exposure which was taken at F.22 on Selochrome pan roll film. *D.J.Dippie.*

Some two and a half months later, on a freezing cold Monday 13th February 1961, we see L1 class 2-6-4T No.67704, designed by Edward Thompson in 1945 for the LNER and built by British Railways at Darlington three years later. It had a working life of just twelve years when withdrawn from Stratford shed in November 1960. The class numbered 100 locomotives, with the prototype being built at Doncaster in 1945, and later batches built by Darlington works, the North British Loco. Co., and Robert Stephenson & Hawthorns. No.67800 was the last to be built in September1950 and, coincidentally, the last to be withdrawn in December1962. Although capable locomotives, they had trouble with motion and hot boxes, and were employed principally across the Eastern and North Eastern regions of the BR network. On visits to North Road, this was the first locomotive seen being cut up in one of the storage lines. The chimney, dome cover, cylinders, rear buffers and hand rails have been removed, and the cutters torches have begun preparing the cab roof and tanks for lifting off. In a few days time the remains would be transferred by rail for melting down to produce new metal products from cars to razor blades. *D.J.Dippie.*

De-tendered D49/2 No.62765 THE GOATHLAND in the company of No.62763 THE FITZWILLIAM await their fate on Monday 13th February 1961. The D49/2s, introduced in 1929 and built at Darlington in 1934, were fitted with Lentz rotary cam poppet valves. It was a development of Gresley's 1927 class D49/1. The Lentz design was intended to assist in starting, and also when the engine was in full gear it would emit a free steam exhaust. 'Hunts' were used to haul seven to ten coach trains on runs of between fifty and a hundred miles. They were progressively replaced by B1s and later by diesel multiple units. No.62765 was withdrawn from Hull Dairycoates on 10th January 1961, less than a month before this picture was taken, and fully disposed of by the end of April. The tenders removed from the D49's found their way to a scrapyard opposite Borough Gardens shed in Gateshead, for scrapping or for re-use in industry. *D.J.Dippie.*

On that dingy Monday in February 1961, David Dippie photographed D49/2 No.62763 THE FITZWILLIAM which was sandwiched between another D49/2 and a B16/1. Having a working life of just twenty-seven years, No.62763 was also built at Darlington in 1934 when it was fitted with the Lentz rotary cam poppet valves. Withdrawn from Dairycoates on 16th January 1961, it used to operate from Hull to York, Leeds, Sheffield, and Scarborough. Although having a reputation for somewhat rough riding, the D49s provided their crews with ample weather protection. It had arrived at North Road scrapyard from Hull in the company of No.62765. Work had not yet commenced on dismantling either engine, as all cab fittings and instruments are still in place. Both locomotives have been separated from their tenders, and No.62763 would be disposed of by the end of March. None of the 'Hunts' survived into preservation, unlike 'Shire' D49/1 No.62712 MORAYSHIRE from which they were developed. *D.J.Dippie.*

With a pair of L1 class 2-6-4Ts for company,   D49/1 62723 NOTTINGHAMSHIRE had arrived at North Road yard coupled to class D49/2s Nos.62763 and 62765 for the journey from Hull Dairycoates, where they were all withdrawn, in January 1961. No.62723 was built at Darlington in 1928 to Gresley's design of the previous year. Although standing in one of the three storage lines, the cutters torch has prepared the cab roof for lifting, and most of the boiler fittings and the motion have been removed. The brass nameplates and cast iron smokebox numberplate and shedcode have taken a lower priority. How times have changed with regard to security. No.62723 would be fully disposed of by the end of February – two weeks hence. *D.J.Dippie.*

Nearside nameplate and splasher of D49/1 No.62723 NOTTINGHAMSHIRE, this 57 inch curved, yellow brass cast nameplate was fitted to Gresley designed LNER Class D49/1 'Shire' 4-4-0 No.327 when it was built at Darlington and entered traffic in July 1928. Shire nameplates were cast in a relatively soft mix of brass, which resulted in them flexing and in some cases fracturing in service. Bolt holes became elongated, and the plate fitted here shows evidence of having required remedial work. The original flush countersunk left hand end bolts have been replaced by through bolts from the rear with nuts fitted at the front. The 9in. x 5in. works numberplate has been removed, probably by a collector, as the one fitted to the offside is still intact (see previous illustration). There are actually four such plates now owned by collectors, and all are believed to have been carried at some time. The original LNER number has been ground off and replaced by a brass strip with the BR number. Shire nameplates were sold as scrap for around £3 to £5 when the engine was withdrawn, but have been sold at auction for up to £16,000 in recent years. *D.J.Dippie.*

The nameplate of D49/2 No.62727 THE QUORN. Built at Darlington in 1929, this engine was named BUCKINGHAMSHIRE from new. It was re-named THE QUORN three years later after the fox hunt operating in an area bordered from a few miles south of Nottingham in the north, to the Leicester City boundary in the south, and from Ashby de la Zouch in the west, to Melton Mowbray in the east. This cast brass left-hand (nearside) nameplate has lost its fox which faced left towards the front of the locomotive. Although both left and right plates were cast identically, the top edge beading was ground away more at the front of the plate to allow clearance for the front paws of the fox which were slightly lower than the back ones. This particular plate was hung for many years in the Great Central Railway museum at Loughborough station before being sold at auction in July 2009 for £11,000. By that time it had been fitted with a replacement fox. Darlington works regularly provided replacement foxes to make complete sets at the time of sale to collectors, and in some cases cast them to facilitate this. These later foxes had a higher copper content than the yellow brass plates, and were not stamped with the LNER locomotive number as found on many of the original foxes. The 9in. x 5in. cast brass works number plate has also been removed, probably by a collector, as it was normal practice at that time for brass and cast iron plates to be left intact until the dismantling process began. *D.J.Dippie.*

February 1961. The remains of D49/1 No.62717 BANFFSHIRE, built Darlington 1928, scrapped Darlington 1961. The 4-4-0 had travelled from Dairycoates shed where it had been withdrawn exactly one month earlier. It now stands in one of North Road's breaking lines in the final stages of disposal, which had been completed by the end of the month. The firebox lagging is totally exposed, at a time when the risk of lung damage by inhalation of the fibres was unknown to the workforce. The cast iron smokebox numberplate would either be melted down, or become one of less than a dozen which are known to have survived into private collections. *D.J.Dippie.*

D49/2 No.62765 THE GOATHLAND, the cast brass right-hand (offside) nameplate has lost its fox which faced right towards the front of the engine. When made at Darlington in October 1934, the plate would have had a cast yellow brass 'rough-haired' fox stamped with the original LNER locomotive number 362 on the reverse. The fox had two half-inch Whitworth studs which passed through the nameplate, and were fastened with nuts which were easily removable. It was works policy at that time to remove foxes for safekeeping before locomotives entered the scrap yard. When plates were later sold to collectors, missing and damaged foxes were replaced from stores. They would not always be the original, and could be rough or smooth haired, stamped or unstamped on the rear, or cast replacements with a slightly higher copper content. Some had been damaged in service by the locomotive crew or cleaners standing on the tail. The 9in. x 5in. cast brass works number plate has been removed, probably by a collector, as locomotives normally arrived at North Road with their brass and cast iron plates still attached. The North Yorkshire village of Goathland latterly achieved fame as the fictional 'Aidensfield' in which the ITV Sunday night drama series 'Heartbeat' was based. A replica of this plate was hung above the fire place in the 'Aidensfield Arms' during filming. *D.J.Dippie.*

Nameplate THE FITZWILLIAM fitted to D49/2 No.62763 was named after a fox hunt which operated in the Peterborough and Oundle areas. The engine was built at Darlington in September 1934 and returned to North Road from Hull Dairycoates some twenty-six years later to be broken up. The cast brass right-hand nameplate is stamped R.359 – right side No.359 – on the area from which the right (front facing) fox has been removed, either by the works for safekeeping as was their policy at the time, or by a collector. The fox would have had the same LNER locomotive number stamped on the rear. Some foxes disappeared in service due to the ease with which the two securing half-inch Whitworth nuts on the rear could be unbolted. This plate was later sold to a collector by British Railways with a replacement fox. The cost of £3-£5 in 1961 made the nameplate a good investment as well as an attractive home decoration, for even in the somewhat depressed Railwayana nameplate market of 2010, it is now worth 1,000 times that amount. *D.J.Dippie.*

A B16/1 class cab side lies in the foreground a stark reminder of what is about to happen to D49/1 No.62723 NOTTINGHAMSHIRE, built at Darlington and entering traffic on 11th July 1928, the 4-4-0 and was initially allocated to York shed. It transferred to Botanic Gardens in Hull some four years later and resided there for a further twenty-seven years before reallocating to its final depot at Dairycoates. It was withdrawn at the Hull shed in January 1961, some four weeks before arriving at North Road. While at Botanic Gardens shed, it worked to Scarborough, Leeds, Doncaster, York and both of the Sheffield stations (Midland) and (Victoria). Typical use would be for hauling trains of seven to ten coaches. Cutting-up has already begun although the locomotive is standing in one of the three storage lines. Concentration was required by BR personnel and enthusiast alike when picking a path around the yard to avoid tripping over the littered scrap items such as the driving and bogie wheels (Q6 drivers and 12 spoke bogies, a trait of Darlington) in the foreground. No.62723 would be fully disposed of by the end of February 1961, after covering a lifetime distance of 1,229,928 miles. *D.J.Dippie.*

Still intact, D49/1 No.62723 NOTTINGHAMSHIRE, on the 13th February 1961 showing cab detail. This side view cab reveals how work is progressing on the dismantling process. The letter 'S' has been chalked on the side to indicate delivery of the locomotive to North Road scrap yard. The sliding glass windows and their wooden frames have been removed, as has the hinged glass cinder screen between the cab windows. On the boiler, the safety valves, whistle and non-ferrous cab fittings and water gauge glasses have gone. The connecting rods have been taken off the crankpins, and the cutters torch has begun the process of separating the lower and upper cab sections before lifting off the roof. In 1961 no thought was given to burning out the loco numbers for collectors, although this would happen in a year or two with a very limited number of Pacific locomotive cab numbers. *D.J.Dippie.*

31

Another view of the mortal remains of D49/1 No.62717 BANFSHIRE along with J25 No.65727. This photograph taken at 12.40 p.m. on 13th February 1961, shows the final stages in disposing of two very different but once proud locomotives. The 'Shire' was built at Darlington in 1928 whilst the 0-6-0 was a 1902 built product of Gateshead. Both had been withdrawn the previous month. They are on the two breaking lines adjacent to North Road station (now the railway museum) in the background, and will shortly have their boilers lifted and transported probably by rail in Weltrol wagons. The smokebox numberplate on the goods engine is fractured and displaced, so will probably be melted down rather than transferred to the stores at Darlington works for sale to a collector for the then scrap price of ten shillings (50p). Apparently none of the Class J25 smokebox numberplates are believed to have survived. *D.J.Dippie.*

The cabside of No.62727. In 1946 this engine was renumbered from 336 to 2727 under the Thompson scheme, and finally it became BR 62727 in August 1950. A long time Starbeck resident (October 1950 to September 1959), it finished its days at Dairycoates. Work will shortly commence on dismantling components, beginning with the safety valves, whistle and then the cladding from the boiler, and the fittings and gauges from the back-head of the firebox. The coupling rods will be removed from the crankpins. The cab windows in their wooden frames will be dismantled, and the hinged glass wind deflectors between the windows will be taken off the cab sides before lifting off the top half of the cab itself. *D.J.Dippie.*

A nice rear end shot of J71 No.68272 which had been built at Darlington almost seventy years earlier by Wilson Worsdell in 1891, and was based on T.W.Worsdell's NER class 'E' of 1886. Standing next to sister engine No.68278, both locomotives had travelled from Thornaby shed a few days earlier. The bunker has been emptied of coal, and the smokebox locking bar rests on the front footplating after cleaning out the ash. The tank side, bunker and cab show signs of unrepaired damage. These two J71s were amongst the last four to be withdrawn, the others being No.68275 (which is next to No.68278 but unseen – see illustration of yard layout as at 13th February 1961 – and No.68233, the final member of the class to be broken up. All four had gone within fifteen days of this photograph being taken. *D.J.Dippie.*

Another resident of Darlington scrap yard on 13th February 1961 was this J71. Made redundant by diesel shunting locomotives, No.68278 had been built at Darlington some sixty-nine years earlier in February 1892 from a Wilson Worsdell design. Unusually, it retains the North Eastern Railway organ pipe whistle. *D.J. Dippie.*

In rather nice condition with the later BR emblem, class Y3 Sentinel No.68160 now renumbered as Departmental Loco No.57 was from a class of thirty-two locomotives introduced in 1927. It had only two speeds, high and low, and was designed by Sentinel Wagon Works, entering traffic in August 1929. No.68160 became Departmental stock in October 1956 when it changed to number 57 from its BR number which it had carried since February 1949. The 9in. x 5in. works number plate carries number 68160 on a 6¾ in. long brass strip overlaid on the original number, and can be seen on the cab side. This engine was in daily use for many years at Dunston Staithes from 6.00 a.m. until 10 p.m. helping coal wagons to gravitate, and was withdrawn in February 1961 from Faverdale works in Darlington. It still carries a Gateshead (52A) shed plate, as it stands in one of North Road's two breaking lines. Note the wrong facing BR crest. *D.J.Dippie.*

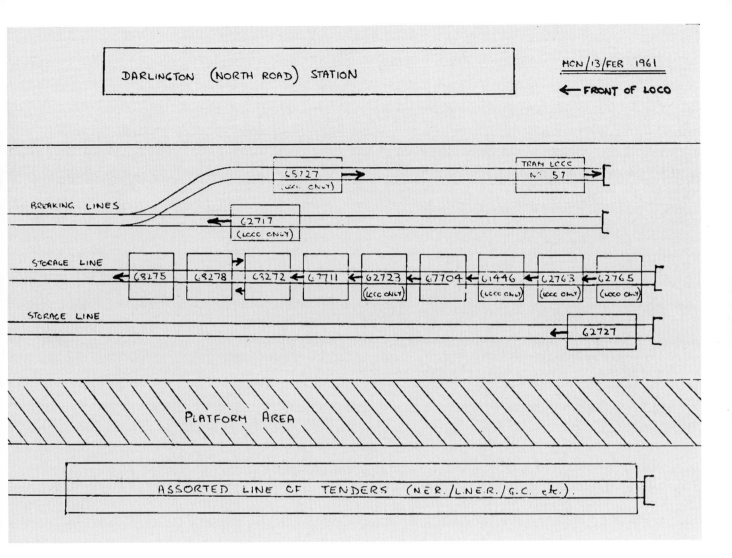

A hand drawn diagram of the situation at Darlington North Road scrap yard on Monday 13th February 1961. Although the layout of the yard had not changed since the previous November, the residents certainly had. *D.J.Dippie.*

Pictured on the 2nd May 1962, was B16/1 No.61413, designed by Vincent Raven for the North Eastern Railway, and built at Darlington in August 1920 as NER No.911, the 4-6-0 was fitted with Stephenson valve gear. It had been withdrawn from the former Lancashire & Yorkshire shed at Mirfield (56D) in September 1961, and had been stored for almost eight months before arriving at North Road. The increase in dieselisation resulted in many of the B16 class spending long periods in store at various depots, often in the open as at York, Neville Hill, Scarborough and Dairycoates. Standing between classmates Nos.61443 and 61415, which were withdrawn at the same time from Mirfield and York respectively, it was not unusual for batches of the same class to arrive and be dismantled together. Whilst the smokebox locking bar lies on the front footplate after ash removal, the tenders have been removed for separate disposal. Cab side windows and their wooden frames have been taken out, as have the glass wind/clinker deflectors fitted between them. Note that the smokebox door has been scorched whilst the brass 9in. x 5in. works number plate has been removed from the front splasher. *D.J.Dippie.*

Seen in North Road's storage sidings in May 1962 is a typical line-up of locomotives headed by J72s Nos.68688 and 68703. Wilson Worsdell designed these shunting locos for the North Eastern Railway in 1898. They were built at Darlington in 1899 and 1914 respectively and both withdrawn in October 1961. Based on Teesside, at Thornaby and West Hartlepool sheds before withdrawal, they were used for goods shunting and local trip workings. The class was widespread throughout the North Eastern Region and in parts of Scotland, and some later replaced J71s on carriage shunting at main stations. They had good power output despite their slender appearance whilst their lifespan varied from sixty-three years, to just eleven for some of the final batch which were completed at Darlington in 1951 for British Railways. *D.J.Dippie.*

At the neck of the yard in this May 1962 illustration we have V3 2-6-2T No.67623. Designed by Nigel Gresley and built at Doncaster in 1931, it had been rebuilt in 1959 from his earlier V1 class. This increased boiler pressure from 180 pounds per square inch to 200 p.s.i. and the tractive effort from 22,464 lb. to 24,960 lb. The locomotive is fitted with front and rear North British type destination board brackets for use on Glasgow suburban services. This is one of the first locomotives I saw in North Road with the overhead electrical warning panels fitted, indicating its use on services operating 'under the wires'. The V3s were competent and popular with enginemen and, although often latterly employed on light duties, were capable of hauling heavy loads with a good turn of speed. No.67623 had been withdrawn four months earlier in January 1962 from Glasgow's Parkhead depot. *D.J.Dippie.*

Standing between an L1 2-6-4T and a J39 0-6-0 on that May day in 1962, is N10 class 0-6-2T No.69097. Introduced by Wilson Worsdell in 1902 for the NER, its design was based on the J25 tender engine and built at Darlington in December 1902. Although used on passenger trains, the N10s were more frequently employed on shunting duties and trip freight workings. No.69097 worked from Bowes Bridge, the only sub-shed of Gateshead, on the Tanfield branch in County Durham. The engine stands in North Road yard awaiting dismantling and is still carrying its cast iron smokebox number plate and 52A shed plate. The locking bar has been removed from the smokebox to facilitate ash cleaning, and the shovel lies on top of the tank. No.69097 worked for almost sixty years before being withdrawn together with Nos.69101 and 69109 on 9th April 1962 from Gateshead. *D.J.Dippie.*

The beautiful lines of Raven 4-6-0 B16/1 No.61429 are shown to good effect in this late September 1961 photograph. It had been withdrawn from Leeds (Neville Hill) shed on 25th September and travelled immediately to Darlington where it was seen in the yard four days later sharing the storage line with another tender and a former GCR 4-6-2T class A5 Pacific tank. Overlooking the scene we have pile of scrap containing the remains of G5 0-4-4T No.67325, formerly of Blaydon shed, which had for many years been sub-shedded at Hexham until displaced to pastures new by the influx of diesel railcars, an A8 bunker and the front end of a J71 languish in the cutting road. *P.J.Robinson.*

Not much remains of J71 class No.68306 on the 17th August 1958, showing the innards of this once proud ex NER locomotive. Exposed are the boiler tubes, firebox stays, reversing lever handle, safety valves and inside motion. No.68306 spent the whole of its working life in the Hartlepools between West, East then West sheds from where it was withdrawn on 14th July 1958. Worthy of note is the steam crane runner truck No.305 behind the 0-6-0T. *I.H.B.Lewis.*

43

r unusual sight of J72 No.68671, from Wrexham shed (6E) in the London Midland Region, fitted with a shorter Connah's Quay-Buckley branch, on which there was a low bridge. Withdrawn from Bidston and sent to Darlington d when it was fitted with a 97L! shed plate is anyone's guess. If anyone can solve this mystery please contact me il or the good old postal service run by the Royal Mail. *P.J.Robinson.*

In November 1960 the unidentified carcass of an ex Great Central Railway A5 4-6-2T still retained both builders' plates – Gorton and LNER. Although built at Gorton, these tank engines attended Darlington for maintenance and of course their demise. Note the wooden sections of the bufferbeam sandwiches fitted to many NER locomotives. *P.J.Robinson.*

On a working Monday in October 1963 we have an ex Great Northern Railway J50 class 0-6-0T shunting a redundant boiler into the scrap yard, alongside the sorry sight of the prototype BR Standard 'Clan' 4-6-2 No.72000 CLAN BUCHANAN with sacked chimney, and J72 No.69021. For various reasons the Polmadie allocated 'Clans' were despised by that depots' footplate men, so in 1958 they were transferred away to Edinburgh, with both Haymarket and St Margarets getting a handful each. However, being used to Gresley's Pacifics, the crews at (64A) and (64B) also loathed the BR lightweight Pacifics and would fail them for the slightest reason. Consequently they were returned to Glasgow and did very little work for the next couple of years, eventually being put into store and thence withdrawal. In England, Kingmoor shed on the other hand used them quite successfully and without complaint! *W.P.Hodgson.*

THE SAD AND HAPPY STORY OF A D20.

In early February 1955, D20 class 4-4-0 No.62383, in BR livery but outwardly in original North Eastern Railway condition, stands forlorn with its boiler condemned lying in the storage line at North Road scrap yard awaiting its fate, or is it! Removed from the yard to the nearby works shortly afterwards, it received a full Heavy Intermediate overhaul, and was coupled to a rebuilt, high-sided NE tender. J.W.Armstrong.

By early April No.62383 stands at the works crossing, immaculately resplendent in her new guise, and awaiting return to her home shed Tweedmouth to work out her final days on the Alnmouth-Newcastle local passenger services. Peeping out behind is Q6 No.63350 awaiting assessment prior to entering shops for a Heavy Intermediate overhaul on 15th April. (*inset*) The only known remains of No.62383 is the 9in.x 5in. brass works plate delivered from Darlington Works cleaned up, cash on delivery, for the princely sum of four shillings and eleven pence – 4/11d (24.5p). *Main picture J.W.Armstrong, inset David Dunn.*

In July 1956 at Killingworth station on the ECML north of Newcastle, No.62383 framed by the footbridge, trundles through the level crossing on the 07-38 a.m. four coach Alnmouth to Newcastle stopping local service. During March 1954 my family moved from Byker to Longbenton, fortunately – for me – there were no schools built locally and I had to attend the nearest which was at Burradon, (a mining village three miles north of Longbenton). The special bus taking us to school stopped at the crossing and this magnificent locomotive, with its massive driving wheels, rolled into the station! And that was me – hooked! A three mile walk every Saturday, armed with a bottle of water and jam butties (known as sandwiches in some circles), I would spend all day sitting on the footbridge watching trains! Worthy of note are the signal box, signals, BR trespass notice, gas lamps and an abundance of telephone wires overhead. *J.W.Armstrong.*

It is now May 1957 and we are, sadly, back in the scrap yard with No.62383 and its fellow class mate No.62375. Our once proud 4-4-0 lies bereft of a tender awaiting her fate with dignity. On No.62375, the splasher and footplate have been cut away to show the Westinghouse pump to good effect, the massive 6ft. 10in. coupled wheels and the twelve-spoked 4ft. bogie wheels. Lying scattered around the yard detritus we have a crank axle, various other axles, dome cover and buffers. Even in the scrap yard No.62383 still holds the elegant lines of a beautiful express locomotive. What price for that smokebox number and shed plate? So now we have the full circle scrap yard, works, running in traffic and back into the scrap yard. What a pity none were preserved, a suggestion was made but British Railways refused, as a North Eastern Railway 4-4-0 was already in the national collection. *P.J.Robinson.*

Stripped of its identification, number, shed and works plates J27 class No.65832 stands like a soldier demoted in disgrace on the 6th June 1966 as if 'bedevilled' by that number 6-6-66! This wonderful workhorse was no longer required after withdrawal from Sunderland shed during the previous March. It spent a couple of months in store before being towed into Northumberland for scrap. *E.Wilson.*

Standing alone and unwanted, one of the two former North Eastern Railway Bo-Bo ES1 electric locomotives – No.26501 – built in 1902 by British Thompson-Houston for the Newcastle Quayside branch. They plied their trade from Manors to the Quayside for the next sixty-two years proving to be extremely efficient. When electric operation ceased on the Quayside branch on 29th February 1964, the two locomotives were stored at South Gosforth car sheds for the next couple of months, thence south to Hellifield shed (24H) until 1966. It was decided to preserve No.26500 but no such luck for No.26501 which was dragged back to the North-East and its demise on 24th July 1966. Fortunately the yard manager at Willoughby's, Paul Humphreys, had the foresight to retain one of the cab sides, which can be seen today in The Blyth & District Model Railway Society clubrooms in North Shields. *L.Rutter.*

Looking immaculate in near ex works condition on 4th August 1967, is Baggage Van M68000M. This vehicle started life in 1957 as South Tyneside Motor Parcels Van E68000 operating the Newcastle to South Shields service. When electric services were withdrawn from that line in January 1963, the Eastleigh-built EMUs went home to the Southern Region and the single parcels van transferred to the London Midland Region becoming M68000M. It found work on the Liverpool-Southport service as a baggage and fish van, notice 'Fish Traffic This End' located at No.2 end of the car, as far away from the driver as possible! Its return to the North-East for dismantling is cloaked in mystery. The only conclusion I can make is that the North Tyneside EMU's were meeting their demise in the yards of Bolckows and Willoughby's, so the scrap men at those places knew how to deal with them or, the e.m.u. was never taken off the NE Region books and simply returned from whence it came! *B.D.Nicholson collection.*

In July 1967 we have a pair of ex NER 0-6-0 class J27 Nos.65872 and 65842, both withdrawn from Sunderland in January, after a lifetime hauling coal trains around the North East. Standing on the top of the firebox of 65842 and cutting away at the boiler tubes, the 'scrapman' is using an oxy-acetylene torch wearing only goggles for protection, oblivious to the dangers of asbestos, I doubt whether he still survives. The pylons in the background convey electricity from Blyth power station away into the distance towards Morpeth. The use of Conflats for shelter is quite apparent to deal with the often inclement local weather. *I.S.Carr.*

The Leviathan partially dismembered, its chimney lying in the foreground. This Stanier 2-8-0 8F No.48148, a long time Lancashire based engine, variously spending its working life at Lancaster (Green Ayre), Heaton Mersey, Newton Heath, Patricroft and then back to Lancaster, where withdrawal and storage took place in June 1965. Pictured on 17th October, it was the only 8F to meet its fate at Choppington. *M.Rutter.*

Willoughby's yard presented quite a line up of motive power on 29th April 1967. The Peppercorn A1 tender off No.60120 KITTIWAKE, J27 No.65842, WD No.90078, J27 No.65872, and Q6s Nos.63405, 63412 and 63450 partially dismantled. Looking towards Bedlington, just this side of the crossing gate is the site of Choppington station, the scrap yard being part of the station yard and now leased from BR. It would take approximately two to three weeks to reduce these engines to useful scrap. *M.Rutter.*

Here shown mutilated in its final form as Departmental No.58 is J72 (No.69005). Built at Darlington in 1949 works No.2086, it was allocated to Gateshead, and did all the usual shunting tasks required of a J72, regularly working as station pilot in Newcastle (Central). After being transferred to Departmental stock and renumbered No.58 it was sent to North Blyth where it resided for the next three years. Upon its withdrawal it spent time in storage at Tyne Dock and Heaton and was eventually despatched to Choppington in early January 1968. Not far from its grave, bereft of cab front and tanks, smokebox toppled off the footplate, its chimney lay split and forlorn whilst the dome cover rests against the level crossing gatepost. Behind lie a Q6 roof and a cylinder block from WD No.90078. The Railway Tavern in the background must have been a magnetic draw for a thirsty workforce. *M.Rutter.*

The last five Gresley V3 2-6-2Ts, Nos.67636, 67684, 67620, 67643 and 67638, lie in Thompson's yard just south of Stockton station circa 1964. These engines, so endemic in the North East, worked anything from local passenger and parcels trains to empty coaching stock between Heaton carriage sidings and Newcastle (Central). Various detail differences with these engines were: two types of outside steam pipes, straight and elbowed, three types of coal space, plated coal rails, plated without rails and hopper, and NB style lamp brackets, and, when new, all were fitted with former North British Railway type destination brackets on the top of the smokebox door and back plate of the bunker. These locomotives had lain in this yard for nearly a year by March 1965; what a shame the preservationists couldn't get their hands on one, possibly due to BR's no resale policy. *I.S.Carr.*

Deviating slightly from the remit of this album, it is worth including this illustration for its rarity. Early in 1976 a complete stranger to the north east of England, a Class 35 (TOPS designation) diesel-hydraulic, Beyer, Peacock built 'Hymek' D7089 in the guise of Departmental No.968005 turned up in Stockton. Built in 1963 at the Gorton, Manchester factory, the B-B Type 3 locomotive had been withdrawn from Bristol (Bath Road) depot in May 1975. It was afterwards used as a coaching stock pre-heating unit at Plymouth before being condemned and finally withdrawn at Plymouth (Laira) in August 1975. How on earth did she get to the North East? Here lying in Phoenix sidings with Stockton station and its wonderful roof, (now long gone) framed by the iron footbridge, she awaits her demise in the adjacent yard. *I.S.Carr.*

ARNOTT YOUNG, FIGHTING COCKS, DINSDALE.

Just past the Fighting Cocks crossing, the reception sidings for Arnott Young's yard contained a pair of Ministry of Supply Riddles designed 'Austerity' War Department 2-8-0s Nos.90207 and 90152, the first a former Western Region engine discerned by the prominent top feed without its cover. It had also been fitted with a home made smokebox numberplate. From 1948 until withdrawal from Rose Grove in August 1965 she served Bristol St Philips Marsh, Southall, Carmarthen and Llanelly before moving north to Gorton then onward to Burnley. *J.W.Armstrong.*

Built by the North British Locomotive Company at their Queens Park works in Glasgow is an example of Peppercorns updated version of Thompson's rebuilt K1/1 MacCAILIN MOR. With works number 26661, K1 2-6-0 No.62057 entered service on 31st November 1949. A useful mixed traffic engine which was allocated new to Darlington, she stayed in the North East for her whole working life which saw it reside at three other sheds: Haverton Hill, York and finally North Blyth. With the remaining members of the class in shocking condition, and supplemented with Ivatt Class 4s, they tottered around local collieries until withdrawal in May 1967. After travelling with a couple 'Clodhoppers' on the final journey to Dinsdale, she is seen here in the reception sidings. *J.W.Armstrong*.

Standing under a crane, Ivatt Class 4 No.43019, with another two for company, await a decision as to where the cutters will begin their job. This is quite a neat and tidy yard compared to the majority of private yards during the heady days of mass destruction. 43019 had quite a chequered career serving from new at: Nottingham, Cricklewood, Stoke, Lower Darwen and finally Sutton Oak from where she was withdrawn in May 1968 before being put into storage at Lostock Hall for three months. Her last journey to Dinsdale took place in early September 1968. *J.W.Armstrong.*

On the banks of the Tyne 16th July 1966, we have the sad remains of steam locomotives previously plying their trade around the many lines in the North East. The photograph shows, in the centre, a cylinder block of a Gresley V2 and a variety of two-to-one motion pieces. Cylinders with their piston rods exposed, remind me of open heart surgery, unfortunately in this case, beyond repair. *K.Gregory.*

Built during the Second World War, in May 1942, Gresley V2 No.3648 spent its career allocated to four different depots: York, Darlington, Thornaby and finally Gateshead from where it was withdrawn as No.60946 in November 1965. After working from York during the conflict with Germany and escaping bombing, it then ends its life in a Gateshead scrap yard on 16th July 1966. The flame cut memento in the company of a loco seat, were possibly a request from an enthusiast. *K.Gregory.*

On the same day as the previous photograph we have another V2, No.60886, which was originally fitted with a one piece mono-block cylinder casting, which was quite expensive to replace, so it was deemed necessary to replace this huge casting with separate cylinder castings, along with outside steam pipes. The transformation at the front end made it impossible for spotters to tell the difference between a V2 and an A3. This was the first engine of this class to receive this treatment at Darlington works in May 1956. It spent most of its life in the North East, a long-time Heaton engine it was finally withdrawn from York in April 1966. With its separated tender, a crane hovers above like a vulture waiting for the imminent death. *K.Gregory.*

Nosing out from behind a pile of scrap and recently uncoupled from its tender, is one of Raven's powerful workhorse Q6 class 0-8-0s No.63429. A Tyne Dock engine, it was frequently seen trundling past Gateshead shed on local coal trains and lasted to near the end of steam on the ER/NER, being withdrawn on the first day of July 1967. Two months later she tries to hide from the cutters torch behind that pile of metal. Also hiding behind the cranes on the right is a redundant Tyneside tugboat. Towering above the works of Vickers Armstrong, the 1960s-built Scotswood Road multi-storeyed flats keep an eye on proceedings. *K.Gregory.*

Through the open gates of Clayton & Davie's yard we can see the prototype Ivatt Class 4 No.43000, standing alone and unwanted, after a career spanning two decades. Allocated firstly to Bletchley shed, followed by Devon's Road in London's East End, then Nuneaton, and finally, as if on inspection of facilities, the three Carlisle engine sheds at Upperby, Canal and Kingmoor in that order prior to retiring to the east coast and North Blyth shed for its last few months working on coal trains to and from the power station at Blyth. *K.Gregory.*

What a sorry sight of a once proud member of the fastest class of steam locomotives in the world. Gresley A4 4-6-2 Pacific 'streak' No.60026 MILES BEEVOR, a long time King's Cross engine and latterly allocated to Aberdeen for use on the three-hour Glasgow services. It is now bereft of its tender, the cods mouth top jaw, dome cover and valve gear. She has just arrived from Crewe works after being cannibalised, and her parts used to complete the preserved engines SIR NIGEL GRESLEY and DOMINION OF CANADA. Now lying at 'Battleship Wharf' buffered between a J27 and a BR Standard Cl.4 (No.75060), with Blyth power station in the foggy distance, she awaits her doom. *M.Rutter.*

The photographer was very fortunate to capture the only ex North British Railway locomotive – J37 0-6-0 No.64595 – to appear and be dealt with inside an English scrap yard. The date is July 1966. Why only one ex NBR locomotive was purchased from Scotland for £2,400 is unclear, as J27 and Q6's were being purchased at that time for lower prices. Perhaps a greater non-ferrous content was promised and this was a trial? This particular engine spent many years of its life in the coalfields of Fife. Discernable in the photograph is Blyth power station and the nose of a Q6. *B.Anderson.*

Overlooking the yard from the east, a slightly panoramic view showing in the distance Blyth power station and the North coal staiths. Berthed at the aptly named 'Battleship Wharf', a redundant warship also in for cutting by Hughes, Bolckow. Central to the scene is Thompson B1 4-6-0 No.61388, recently arrived from Low Moor (Bradford) shed. Behind the B1 is a locally based J27 and in front K1 No.62060 which was new in from Tyne Dock shed. Above the K1 we have a set of North Tyneside electric units made redundant by DMUs and the cranes waiting intently for their job to begin. In the foreground are lines of empty hoppers waiting to be taken to North East collieries to be filled with coal. *M.Rutter.*

The public road in front of Bolckows establishment allowed access for viewing into the yard or over the fence. Looking directly west, we see one of the four Standard Class 2 2-6-2Ts, No.84001, recently withdrawn from Llandudno Junction shed in October 1964, and now residing in the yard prior to cutting up in January 1965. These 2-6-2Ts were built between Crewe and Darlington for use on the Midland and Southern regions but had a relatively short life owing to the influx of DMUs. Rather an unusual visitor to the North East, albeit the Darlington built ones worked on running in turns in the South Durham Area. *M.Rutter.*

A strangely disorientated view captured on film in November 1967 of the cab of WD 'Austerity' No.90009 taken from the upturned roof of a North Tyneside electric unit. A notice adhering to 'No Smoking' adorns the carriage end, and on the left side of the door top is the red communication handle. Adjacent to 90009's cab are two spring loaded seats, which were quite useful on crowded coastal trains. Many a happy day was spent at the seaside as a young boy, travelling from Heaton to Cullercoats and passing Heaton shed, a joy for the young spotter. *M.Rutter.*

Hiding behind buildings situated within the yard, we have a most unusual visitor to the North East in the shape of BR Standard Class 4 4-6-0 No.75060, purchased from Croes Newydd (Wrexham) by H,B for £1,865 on 14th September 1967 and pictured some three weeks later on 8th October. Allocated to former LMS lines depots at Leicester (15C), Derby (17A), Aintree (8L), Edge Hill (8A) and finally Croes Newydd (6C), it had not previously worked anywhere in the North East. *M.Rutter.*